NAVIGATING MIDDLE SCHOOL

A GUIDE TO FRIENDSHIP, GROWTH, AND SELF-DISCOVERY

DR. ROGER M. JACK

ISBN: 979-8-9907029-3-6
Independently published.
Jack & Co. Press

To my beloved wife Leslie and my three incredible sons, Micah, Roman, and Tatum. Your unwavering support and endless love have fueled my journey every step of the way. To all my remarkable students, those from refugee camps in Somalia and Kenya to international learners across Europe and Asia, and ESL students spanning from South to Central America, as well as countless others from Maine to New Jersey, you are the heartbeat of this book.

CONTENTS

RESOURCES BY CHAPTERS

WELCOME TO MIDDLE SCHOOL

1. Your School website
2. Teen Programs at Your School or local Library
3. Headspace - https://www.headspace.com/
4. The American Middle School Association (AMLE) – www.amle.org
5. www.kidshealth.org

BUILDING HEALTHY FRIENDSHIPS

1. Youth Groups
2. Counseling and Guidance Services
3. Online Learning Platforms (consult with parents and counselors)
4. Teens Against Bullying – www.pacerteensagainstbullying.org

NURTURING SELF-ESTEEM

1. Inspirational Podcasts and Videos
2. Counseling and Guidance Services
3. Confidence-Building Workshops
4. Positive Parenting, Thriving Kids – https://childmind.org/

EXPLORING PERSONAL GROWTH

1. Goal-Setting Apps
2. Online Learning Platforms (consult with parents and counselors)
3. Youth Groups
4. Counseling and Guidance Services

HANDLING DRAMA & CONFLICT

1. National Conflict Resolution Center (NCRC) – https://ncrconline.com/
2. Teens Against Bullying – www.pacerteensagainstbullying.org
3. StopBullying.gov – www.stopbullying.gov
4. Kids Helpline 1-800-668-6868

THE WORLD OF DATING

1. Kids Helpline 1-800-668-6868
2. www.teenlineonline.org
3. https://kidshealth.org/

BALANCING ACADEMICS & FUN

1. My Study Life – www.mystudylife.com
2. Time Management for Teens – Book (A number of options on Amazon)
3. Mindfulness for Teens – www.mindfulnessforteens.com
4. Khan Academy – www.khanacademy.org

COPING WITH STRESS & ANXIETY

1. American Psychological Association – www.apa.org
2. Mindfulness for Teens – www.mindfulnessforteens.com
3. Teen Mental Health – www.teenmentalhealth.org
4. National Alliance on Mental Illness (NAMI) – www.nami.org

PREPARING FOR HIGH SCHOOL

1. High School Transition Tips – https://www.amle.org/transition-to-high-school-the-student-perspective/
2. College Board – www.collegeboard.org
3. TeenLife – https://www.teenlife.com/
4. Mindset Works – www.mindsetworks.com

STAYING CONNECTED

1. LinkedIn for Students – https://students.linkedin.com/content/me/students/en-us
2. Toastmasters International – www.toastmasters.org
3. Future Business Leaders of America (FBLA) – www.fbla-pbl.org

INTRODUCTION

My journey to becoming an educator was as unexpected as it was transformative. After earning my bachelor's degree in film from Brooklyn College, NY, I found myself moving to Maine—a place with few opportunities for a film career. It was here, amid the search for meaningful work, that I stumbled upon a path that would define the next two decades of my life: teaching.

It began with a simple step into the world of middle school as a soccer coach, followed by substitute teaching across the state, and eventually a role as a special education classroom assistant. The turning point came when our school welcomed a group of Somali refugees who were unschooled having spent their childhoods in Kenyan refugee camps. Despite my background in film, not education, I was thrust into a teaching position when the need arose—a challenge I accepted with trepidation but which ultimately led me to discover my passion for teaching middle school.

But my journey didn't stop there. Guided by my faith and a commitment to making a difference, I furthered my education by earning a master's degree in education and a doctorate in educational leadership. These achievements not only deepened my understanding of educational systems but also cemented my role as an advo-

1

cate for students facing challenges—from racism and overcrowded ESL classes to the struggles inherent in adapting to a new country and an unwelcoming city.

Throughout my career, whether as a teacher or an administrator, middle school has held a special place in my heart. It's an age of boundless curiosity and of significant growth as well as a time when the foundations for future success are laid. This book was born from over two decades of experience in education, both pre- and post-pandemic, and aims to assist students as they navigate the evolving landscape of middle school. It's an attempt to address the hurdles that students will face and is enriched by my experiences and the deep belief that, with the right guidance, every middle schooler can thrive.

Middle school can indeed be a wonderful place filled with learning, discovery, and joy. But it also comes with its share of challenges. Through this guide, I hope to offer strategies, insights, and encouragement to help you navigate these crucial years. Drawing on my faith, educational background, and firsthand experience as both a teacher and an administrator, I aim to prepare you for the journey ahead.

Welcome to the adventure of middle school. Let this book, which offers lessons learned from decades of dedication to education, be your guide through its halls. Here's to embracing every moment of your middle school journey with hope, resilience, and an open heart.

WELCOME

As you turn the pages of this book and embark on the activities within, remember you are on an incredible journey—one filled with discovery, growth, and endless possibilities. Middle school is a unique chapter in your life. It's a time when you're starting to find your place in the world and learning more about who you are and who you want to be.

There will be days filled with laughter and triumph, and there will be days that challenge you in ways you didn't expect. Embrace them all. Each experience, whether a success or a setback, is a stepping stone on your path to becoming the amazing individual you are meant to be. Think of every situation as a learning opportunity.

Know that you are not alone. Surround yourself with friends and mentors who uplift you, and don't hesitate to lean on them when the going gets tough. Your family, teachers, spiritual leader, and friends are your team, and they are cheering you on every step of the way.

Above all, remember to be kind—to others and

yourself. The world is a better place because you are in it, bringing your unique light and perspective to those around you. Your kindness, your dreams, and your actions have the power to make a positive impact. Go with the changes and change with them into a better human being.

Hold on to hope, even in moments of doubt. The challenges you face today are preparing you for a bright future, one where you can achieve anything you set your mind to. Believe in yourself and your ability to overcome obstacles. You have so much strength and potential within you just waiting to be unleashed.

And finally, know that you are loved. You are valued for exactly who you are, and there is a whole community of people ready to support you and celebrate your journey.

So take a deep breath, step forward with courage, and embrace the adventure of middle school. This is your time to shine, to learn, and to grow. We can't wait to see all the wonderful things you will do.

With all my encouragement, hope, and love,

Dr. Roger M. Jack

Your Guide Through Middle School

P.S. Have faith, hope, and love, but above all, love!

Chapter 1

Introduction to Welcome to Middle School

- Brief introduction to the chapter
- Overview of what middle school is like

Setting the Scene for Middle School

- Description of the typical middle school environment
- Changes from elementary school to middle school
- Introduction of new challenges and opportunities

Adapting to New Experiences

- Tips on adapting to new routines and environments
- Emphasis on the importance of being open to change

Real Stories: Transitioning to Middle School

- Anonymized stories from students about their first experiences in middle school

Expert Advice: Understanding Middle School Challenges

- Insights from psychologists and educators on common challenges
- Advice on how to navigate these challenges effectively

Activities and Reflections

- Interactive exercises for self-reflection
- Journaling section with prompts related to adapting to middle school

Personalization Space and Resource Directory

- Encouraging personalization of the guide
- A list of resources for additional support

CHAPTER ONE

WELCOME TO MIDDLE SCHOOL

This guide is your companion through an exciting phase of your life. Middle school is not just another step in your educational journey; it's a world full of new experiences, friendships, challenges, and discoveries about who you are and want to become.

This first chapter will set the stage for your middle school adventure. You'll learn what to expect, how things might differ from what you're used to, and most importantly, how to adapt and thrive in this new environment. Middle school is a time of significant changes—not just in your studies but in your social life, your emotions, and your view of the world. It's a period when friendships become more complex, interests diverge, and you start forming your unique identity.

But don't worry; you're not alone on this journey. Along the way, you'll find stories from students who have been in your shoes, pro tips from decades of experience, and activities that will help you reflect on and navigate these exciting years. There's also space for you to make this guide your own. Through notes, drawings, or stickers, you can personalize it and make it a true reflection of your middle school experience.

So take a deep breath, open your mind, and get ready to embark on an incredible journey of growth, friendship, and self-discovery. Welcome to middle school!

SETTING THE SCENE FOR MIDDLE SCHOOL

Middle school is a vibrant, bustling world distinct from the familiar corridors of elementary school. Here, a diverse mix of students fill the halls as they each set out on their quests for self-discovery. This is a place where you'll encounter a range of subjects, new teachers, and various extracurricular activities that cater to every imaginable interest.

One of the most noticeable changes is the structure of your day. Unlike elementary school, where one teacher might have guided you through most subjects, middle school introduces the concept of changing classrooms and teachers for different subjects. This shift adds variety to your day and helps you develop organizational skills as you manage different expectations from multiple teachers.

Pro tip: You'll probably find yourself comparing your old school to your new one, your old teachers to your new teachers, and what you're used to with the changes you're now facing. But here's the thing: the sooner you embrace your new school and all the new experiences that come with it, the quicker you'll adjust and thrive.

Middle school also brings greater academic challenges. The coursework becomes more complex and requires a higher level of critical thinking. You'll learn to juggle multiple assignments, tests, and projects, each demanding attention and effort. It's a step up but also an opportunity to discover subjects you're passionate about and talents you didn't know you had.

Socially, middle school is a tapestry of evolving relationships. Friendships deepen, new ones form, and some may fade away as interests and classes differ. It's a time to explore friendships that complement your evolving interests and values. Remember, it's normal for social circles to change during this period, and it's an integral part of finding out where you fit in.

Middle school is also where many students begin to form their identities. You'll have opportunities to join clubs, sports teams, or arts programs, each offering a chance to explore different facets of your personality and interests. It's a time to be curious, try new things, and discover what excites you to learn and grow. You'll also be exposed to many "new" things that shouldn't be present in middle school, like public displays of affection (PDA): kids hugging, holding hands, occasionally sneaking a kiss in a corner somewhere, and incessant touching. You'll come to understand that there are students your age who vape and even use marijuana and drink alcohol—not necessarily in school, but sometimes.

As you navigate this new landscape, you'll learn valuable life skills, such as time management, resilience, and self-advocacy. These skills are not just necessary for school but for life in general. Middle school is more than a stepping stone to high school; it's a foundation for your future.

This chapter will explore ways to adapt to these changes, embrace new opportunities, and make the most of your middle school years. Remember, every student's experience is unique, but the challenges and triumphs you face will help shape the person you're becoming.

ADAPTING TO NEW EXPERIENCES

Stepping into middle school is like loading a fantastic new game like Minecraft Dungeons—it's exciting, a bit challenging, but oh-so rewarding once you get the hang of it. Let's talk about how you can level up in this new adventure.

First off, remember that everyone is a newbie at this. Even those who seem to have it all figured out are trying to find their groove. It's totally okay to feel lost or overwhelmed at first.

Getting the Schedule Down: Middle school is like a puzzle—you have different classes in different rooms with other teachers. It might sound like a lot, but you'll get the hang of it.

Pro tip: Keep a copy of your schedule in your locker, snap a pic on your phone if phones are permitted, or check your schedule on your Chromebook or laptop before your next class.

Making New Friends: Think of middle school as a colossal meet-up. You'll see kids from different schools and backgrounds, and that's your chance to make some epic new friends. Remember, everyone's looking to fit in; so don't be shy about saying "hi" to any brand new students sitting where you once sat.

Dealing with Homework: Yeah, the homework scene steps up a notch here. But don't sweat it. Break it into chunks, just like tackling levels in a game. Set small goals, and you'll be acing them before you know it.

Join the Club: Whether you're into sports, music, art, or coding, there's probably a club for that. Clubs are like cheat codes for making friends with the same interests. Plus, it's super fun to do stuff you love with others who love it too.

Stay True to You: Middle school is when you'll hear a lot about 'fitting in.' But here's the thing: being yourself is your superpower. Embrace what makes you unique, and you'll attract friends who dig the real you.

Remember, adapting to middle school is a journey, not a race. Take it one day at a time, keep an open mind, and have fun exploring this new world. You've got this!

REAL STORIES: TRANSITIONING TO MIDDLE SCHOOL

In this part, we're diving into real-deal stories from kids who've already ridden the middle school rollercoaster. These stories are from students like you who faced everything middle school threw at them and became stronger!

STORY 1: THE FIRST DAY FRENZY

Emily, now in 8th grade, remembers her first day in 6th grade. "I was super nervous and got lost twice trying to find my science class. I thought I'd never figure it out. But then I met Jake, who was lost too. We ended up finding the class together and becoming besties. Funny how a crazy moment turned into an awesome friendship."

STORY 2: HOMEWORK OVERLOAD

Kevin, a 7th grader, talks about his struggle with homework. "I thought I was drowning in homework during the first week. I was staying up late and still not getting it all done. Then, my sister showed me how to break it down into smaller tasks and set priorities. It worked, and now I'm handling it like a pro."

STORY 3: FINDING MY CREW

Alisha, now in high school, reflects on her middle school days. "I was shy and thought I'd never find friends who 'got' me. But then I joined the drama club, and everything changed. I met people who were just as quirky and fun as I am. We're still friends, even though we're in different schools now."

These stories show that it's normal to feel lost or overwhelmed initially. But they also prove that you'll find your way, make incredible friends, and learn a ton about handling new challenges. Remember, every middle schooler's story is unique, and yours is just beginning!

EXPERT ADVICE: UNDERSTANDING MIDDLE SCHOOL CHALLENGES

Now, let's hear some wisdom from the pros—psychologists, teachers, and folks who know what's up with the middle school scene. They have some cool insights and tips to help you navigate this new world.

EXPERT 1: THE PSYCHOLOGY OF CHANGE

Dr. Lopez, a psychologist who works with middle schoolers, says, "Middle school is a big transition, and it's normal to feel a mix of excitement and nervousness. The key is understanding that change is a part of life and that learning to adapt is a super skill. Don't be afraid to ask for help if you feel overwhelmed."

EXPERT 2: ACADEMIC ADJUSTMENTS

Ms. Patel, a middle school teacher, offers this advice: "The jump in academic demands can be a shock. But remember, it's okay not to get everything right the first time. Learning is about making mistakes and growing. Stay organized, and don't hesitate to talk to your teachers if you're struggling—we're here to help!"

EXPERT 3: SOCIAL SMARTS

Mr. Thompson, a school counselor, highlights social changes. "Middle school is when friendships can shift, and that's okay. It's a time to explore and find people who share your interests and values. Be kind, be yourself, and don't feel pressured to fit into a mold. True friends are those who appreciate you for who you are."

These experts remind us that middle school is a learning curve. It's not just about grades and classes; it's about developing life skills, like resilience, adaptability, and empathy. Remember their advice as you navigate your middle school journey, and don't forget—you've got a whole team of adults in your corner, cheering you on!

ACTIVITIES AND REFLECTIONS

ACTIVITY 1: YOUR MIDDLE SCHOOL MAP

Draw a map of your middle school life. Include your classes, your favorite hangout spots, and where you find challenges. Use symbols and colors to represent different feelings and experiences. This map is a fun way to visualize your school journey!

REFLECTION 1: NEW BEGINNINGS

In the journal space provided, answer these questions:

1) What are you most excited about in middle school?

2) What are you nervous about?

3) How can you overcome these challenges?

ACTIVITY 2: FRIENDSHIP GOALS

List the qualities you value in a friend. Next, think about how you can be that kind of friend to others. Remember, friendship is a two-way street!

-
-
-
-
-
-
-

-
-
-
-
-
-

_____

_____

_____

_____

_____

_____

_____

_____

_____

REFLECTION 2: EMBRACING CHANGE

Reflect on a significant change you've experienced before. How did you adapt? What did you learn? Write down your thoughts. This reflection can help you see how capable you are of handling change.

_____

_____

_____

_____

_____

_____

_____

_____

_____

_____

_____

_____

_____

_____

_____

_____

_____

_____

DOODLE CANVAS: LET YOUR PEN ROAM FREE!

Explore. Experiment. Express.

The focus of this guide is you! You can draw, write, paste your favorite stickers, or record special moments in this space. Make it reflect your individuality!

RESOURCE LIST

- **Visit your school's website** to access resources, club information, and updates about your school.
- **Teen Programs at your local library:** Look at what your library offers, including tech workshops and book clubs.
- **'Headspace'** and other mindfulness apps are great for guided relaxation and stress reduction.
- **The American Middle School Association (AMLE)** offers middle school students, parents, and educators tools and assistance (www.amle.org).
- At **www.kidshealth.org,** you'll find Nemours KidsHealth guides for managing social dynamics and academic obstacles during the middle school years.

Keep in mind that these tools are there to assist you as you navigate middle school. There's always someone or something to help, whether you need assistance, wish to pursue new hobbies, or need someone to chat with.

Chapter 2

Introduction to Building Healthy Friendships

- Brief overview of the importance of friendships in middle school
- Introduction to the concepts of different personalities and building relationships

Understanding Different Personalities

- Explanation of various personality types students might encounter
- Tips on how to understand and appreciate diverse personalities

Making New Friends

- Strategies and tips for initiating friendships
- Importance of shared interests and being oneself

Maintaining Friendships

- Advice on nurturing and maintaining friendships
- Emphasis on communication, respect, and shared activities

Navigating Conflicts and Misunderstandings

- Guidance on how to deal with conflicts in friendships
- Importance of empathy, listening, and problem-solving

Real Stories: Friendship Journeys

- Anonymized stories from students about navigating friendship dynamics

Activities and Reflections

- Interactive exercises related to building and maintaining friendships
- Journaling prompts focused on personal experiences with friends

Personalization Space and Resource Directory

- Encouragement for students to personalize the guide
- A list of resources for additional advice and support in friendship matters

CHAPTER TWO

BUILDING HEALTHY RELATIONSHIPS

A good friend can sometimes stick closer than a brother or sister. It is no understatement that a true friend can be a great source of comfort, support, and guidance; friendship is one of school's coolest and most important aspects.

Friendships during middle school are like unlocking new levels in a game; they can be fun, challenging, and super rewarding. Here, you'll meet folks from all walks of life, each with unique personalities. Understanding these different personalities can help you make new friends and keep those friendships strong.

But hey, let's be real—making and maintaining friends isn't always a walk in the park. There's no 'one-size-fits-all' approach because everyone is different. Sometimes, you might face misunderstandings or conflicts, and that's okay. It's all part of learning how to build healthy, lasting friendships.

In this chapter, you'll discover tips for making new friends, ways to keep your friendships going strong, and how to smooth over any rough patches. We've also got some cool activities, stories from other students, and pro tips to guide you along the way.

Are you ready to dive in? Let's begin this exciting journey of building connections that could last a lifetime!

UNDERSTANDING DIFFERENT PERSONALITIES

Middle school is like a giant melting pot of personalities. You'll meet the quiet ones, the class clowns, the bookworms, the athletes, and so many more. It's like a real-life version of a social network that is buzzing with all sorts of characters. Understanding these different personalities is key to building great friendships.

1. **The Quiet Ones:** These friends might not be the loudest in the room, but they often have deep thoughts and cool ideas.

> Pro tip: Try having one-on-one conversations with them; you might be surprised at how much you have in common.

2. **The Class Clowns:** Always ready with a joke, these friends can be super fun. But remember, sometimes they need a serious friend to talk to when the laughter fades.

3. **The Bookworms:** If you love stories or learning new things, these friends can take you on epic intellectual adventures. Don't judge a book by its cover; these pals often have fascinating insights and hobbies.

4. **The Athletes:** Into sports? These friends are all about teamwork and energy. Even if you're not sporty, their determination and spirit can be super inspiring.

5. **The Artists and Musicians:** Creative and often passionate, these friends can introduce you to the world of art and music. Their perspective on life can be refreshingly different.

Understanding these personalities isn't about putting people into boxes. It's about appreciating what makes each person unique. Everyone has a story, a hobby, or a joke that can add something special to your day.

TIPS FOR CONNECTING

- **Be Open-Minded:** Give everyone a chance. Sometimes, the best friendships come from the most unexpected places.
- **Ask Questions:** Show interest in what others love. It's a great way to

start conversations.

- **Share About Yourself:** Friendships are a two-way street. Don't be afraid to open up about your interests, too.

Middle school friendships are about exploring these different personalities and learning from each other. Be curious, be kind, and get ready to meet some amazing people on your middle school journey!

MAKING NEW FRIENDS

Stepping into middle school is like entering a whole new world of opportunities to make friends. But sometimes, the 'friendship quest' can feel a bit like a maze. Don't worry; here are some cheat codes to help you navigate it!

1. **Join the Club:** Literally! Whether it's sports, drama, chess, or robotics, clubs are awesome for meeting people who share your interests. It's like joining a team in a game where everyone's on the same quest.

2. **Be a Conversation Starter:** Got a classmate who's always drawing cool stuff? Compliment them and ask about their art. Notice someone reading your favorite book? That's your conversation starter right there. Remember, a simple "Hi" can lead to a hundred stories.

3. **Group Projects:** They might seem daunting, but group projects are great for making friends. You get to collaborate and share ideas, which is a cool way to bond.

4. **Lunch Time:** Lunchtime is not just for eating; it's prime time for socializing. Join a table or invite someone to sit with you. It's a casual way to chat and get to know your classmates.

5. **Be Yourself:** This is the golden rule. You're at your best when

you're being genuine. Friends who like you for who you are, are the friends you want to keep.

Remember, making friends is about quality, not quantity. It's about finding those few special people who get you and with whom you can be your true self. Take a deep breath, be brave, and start building those awesome friendships that could last a lifetime!

MAINTAINING FRIENDSHIPS

Okay, so you've made some cool new friends. High five! But, like a garden, friendships need care to grow. Here's how to keep your friend-ship garden flourishing:

1. **Stay Connected:** Life gets busy, but try to keep in touch. Texts, calls, or even old-school notes passed in class (just be sneaky about it) can keep the friendship vibe strong.

2. **Quality Time:** Hang out! Plan a movie night, ride a bike, or just chill at the park. It's these fun times that build lasting memo-ries.

3. **Be a Good Listener:** Sometimes, your friend might need some-one to talk to. Be that person who listens, not just with your ears but your heart.

4. **Celebrate Their Wins:** Got a friend who aced a test or scored a goal? Cheer for them! It's awesome to know someone's got your back.

5. **Be Honest and Respectful:** True friends are honest, even when it's tough. But remember, it's not just what you say; it's how you say it. Respect and kindness go a long way.

6. **Give Space When Needed:** Everyone needs alone time. If your friend needs space, it's cool. It doesn't mean they don't want to

be friends anymore.

Friendships in middle school can at times feel like a roller coaster—exciting, sometimes unpredictable, but always worth the ride. Remember these tips, and you'll have a squad that sticks together through thick and thin.

NAVIGATING CONFLICTS AND MISUNDERSTANDINGS

Let's face it: misunderstandings and disagreements happen even in the best friendships. It's like hitting a glitch in a game—frustrating but fixable. Here's how to smooth things out and get back to having fun together.

1. **Keep Calm and Talk It Out:** Feeling upset? Take a breather first. When you're ready, talk to your friend calmly about what's bothering you. It's like hitting the pause button before tackling the next level.

2. **Listen to Their Side:** Remember, every story has two sides. Give your friend a chance to share their perspective. It's not just about hearing their words but understanding their feelings.

3. **Apologize When Necessary:** If you mess up, own it. A sincere "I'm sorry" can do wonders. It shows that you're responsible and care about your friend's feelings.

> Pro tip: After apologizing, try not to repeat the same mistake again.

4. **Agree to Disagree:** Not every disagreement needs a winner. Sometimes, agreeing to disagree is the best way to move forward.

5. **Seek Help if Needed:** Stuck in a tough spot? It's okay to ask a trusted adult for advice. Sometimes, a little guidance is all you need to clear up the confusion.

Overcoming conflicts can make your friendship stronger. It's like leveling up in understanding and respect for each other. Don't let a little bump in the road end a great friendship. Work it out, and you'll be back to laughing and having a blast in no time!

> Pro tip: When navigating conflict and misunderstanding, it's best not to share the conflict with a bunch of students or talk about it within earshot of others who aren't trusted adults or close friends.

REAL STORIES: FRIENDSHIP JOURNEYS

The following section explores how students like you navigate the ups and downs of friendships. These stories highlight the importance of communication, boundaries, and understanding in building and maintaining healthy relationships.

STORY 1: SETTING BOUNDARIES

Kayla was always there for her friends, even when they were in the middle of drama. She would listen, try to help, and mediate some of the conflict. However, she soon realized that she was becoming exhausted from always giving to her friends and not receiving anything back, so she stopped and found a guidance counselor who helped her establish boundaries with her friends and take better care of herself.

STORY 2: CLEARING UP MISUNDERSTANDINGS

Genny and Aya were best friends in 7th grade who shared everything and kept each other's secrets. That suddenly changed when a rumor started that Genny was talking behind Aya's back. The two decided to sit down and talk it out without the audience of their other friends and realized that it was a complete misunderstanding.

STORY 3: TURNING RIVALS INTO FRIENDS

Eighth graders Shawn and Lucas were incredibly competitive. They both played basketball, soccer, and football. They often saw each other as rivals even though they had never had a real conversation in the past; they just assumed this position of being enemies. They were placed in the same science group working on a volcano project and discovered that they had the same work ethic and other things in common. They soon became close friends.

Building healthy friendships takes effort and understanding, as demonstrated by these stories. By setting boundaries, clearing up mis-understandings, and being open to new connections, you can create strong and supportive relationships.

ACTIVITIES AND REFLECTIONS

ACTIVITY 1: FRIENDSHIP TREE

Draw a tree and label each branch with the name of a friend. On the leaves, write down the qualities you appreciate in each friend. This visual can remind you of the wonderful people in your life and what makes each friendship special.

REFLECTION 1: A FRIEND IN NEED

Think of a time when a friend helped you out. Write about how it made you feel and why that moment was important. This reflection helps you appreciate the value of friendship during tough times.

_____

_____

_____

_____

_____

_____

_____

_____

_____

_____

_____

_____

_____

_____

_____

_____

_____

ACTIVITY 2: ROLE REVERSAL

Imagine you're in your friend's shoes during a disagreement. Write down how you think they felt and why. This activity helps you develop empathy and understand conflicts from both sides.

_____

_____

_____

_____

_____

_____

_____

_____

_____

_____

_____

_____

_____

_____

_____

REFLECTION 2: GROWING TOGETHER

Reflect on a friendship that has changed or grown over time. What made it stronger? What challenges did you overcome together? Understanding these dynamics can help you maintain and nurture your friendships.

_____

_____

_____

_____

_____

_____

_____

_____

_____

_____

_____

_____

_____

_____

_____

DOODLE CANVAS: LET YOUR PEN ROAM FREE!

Explore. Experiment. Express.

The focus of this guide is you! You can draw, write, paste your favorite stickers, or record special moments in this space. Make it reflect your individuality!

RESOURCE LIST

- **Youth Groups:** Connect with local youth groups at religious or community centers for spiritual growth and fellowship.
- **Counseling and Guidance Services:** Reach out to school counselors or local faith-based organizations for guidance in friendships and personal development.
- **Online Learning Platforms:** Safe, moderated online forums for teens to discuss faith and friendships.
- **Teens Against Bullying:** Offers resources for students, parents, and educators on bullying prevention and building healthy relationships (www.pacerteensagainstbullying.org).

These resources provide support and guidance in navigating your middle school friendships. Remember, you're never alone; there's always help and guidance available.

Chapter 3

Introduction to Nurturing Self-Esteem

- Brief overview of the concept of self-esteem
- Emphasis on the importance of self-confidence in middle school

Embracing Individuality

- Exploring the importance of accepting and celebrating one's uniqueness
- Tips on how to appreciate and embrace individual differences

Boosting Self-Confidence

- Practical strategies for enhancing self-confidence
- The role of positive self-talk and setting achievable goals

Overcoming Self-Doubt

- Understanding and addressing the causes of self-doubt
- Techniques for transforming self-doubt into positive action

Real Stories: Discovering Your Inner Strength

- Anonymized stories from students about finding their confidence

Activities and Reflections

- Interactive exercises for building self-esteem and confidence
- Journaling prompts to encourage self-reflection and personal growth

Personalization Space and Resource Directory

- Space for students to personalize their guide with their thoughts and experiences
- A directory of resources for further support in nurturing self-esteem

CHAPTER THREE

NURTURING SELF-ESTEEM

In middle school, you may experiment with different responses to situations as you build your confidence in who you are. This chapter is about one of the most important things you'll ever wear—your self-esteem. It's not a shirt or a cool pair of shoes, but it's something that makes you feel just as good, if not better!

Self-esteem is how you see and value yourself. It's like the foundation of a house—the stronger it is, the more solid and resilient the house is to whatever weather comes its way. In middle school, where everything is changing—your body, your emotions, and your social life—having strong self-esteem is super important.

But hey, boosting your self-esteem isn't always easy. Sometimes, you might feel like you're not good enough, or you may start comparing yourself with others. That's totally normal, but remember: you're unique and awesome in your own way. The following information will guide you through embracing your individuality, boosting your confidence, and overcoming any self-doubt.

You'll find cool activities, stories from other students, and advice that can help you feel more confident and sure about who you are. Get ready to dive into a journey of self-discovery and empowerment. You're about to learn how to shine with confidence!

EMBRACING INDIVIDUALITY

Middle school is like a giant canvas, and you're the artist. Your individuality is your unique color palette—no one else has the same combination of colors (or qualities) as you. Embracing this individuality is key to painting a middle school experience that's vibrant, authentic, and truly your own.

Pro tip: Middle school is the time when you start forming your own thoughts, opinions, emotions, and values, which might not always align with what you've learned at home. And that's totally okay. By having open conversations with your family, you can find a balance that respects both your beliefs and theirs, helping you build a stronger sense of self-esteem and understanding.

Celebrate What Makes You 'You': Maybe you love science fiction, play the trombone, or have a knack for telling jokes. Whatever your thing is, own it! Your hobbies, interests, and quirks make you special.

Resist the Comparison Trap: It's easy to look at others and feel like you don't measure up. But remember, comparing yourself to others is like comparing apples and oranges—both are great, just different.

Find Your Tribe: Look for friends who appreciate and celebrate your uniqueness. These are the people who will cheer you on and enjoy the special blend of talents and quirks you bring to the table.

Explore and Experiment: Middle school is the perfect time to try new things. Join clubs, pick up a new hobby, or learn a skill you've always been curious about. This is how you discover new facets about yourself.

Reflect on Your Strengths: Take time to think about what you're good at and what you enjoy. These strengths are a big part of what makes you amazing.

Remember, embracing your individuality is about being comfortable and confident in who you are. It's about not being afraid to stand out and be different, because that's what makes you, well, you! In a world where everyone is trying to fit in, the bravest thing you can do is stand out.

BOOSTING SELF-CONFIDENCE

Self-confidence is like a muscle—the more you use it, the stronger it gets. Here are some power moves to help you build your confidence muscle in middle school:

1. **Positive Self-Talk:** Your words have power, especially the ones you say to yourself. Instead of thinking, "I can't do this," say, "I'll do my best." Changing your inner dialogue can boost your confidence.

2. **Set Achievable Goals:** Start with small goals, like participating in class or trying a new activity. Achieving these can give you a real confidence boost and motivate you to take on bigger challenges.

3. **Celebrate Your Wins:** Got a good grade or finally mastered that tough piano piece? Celebrate it! Recognizing your achievements, no matter how small they are, is a great way to feel good about yourself.

4. **Learn from Mistakes:** Everyone messes up sometimes—it's part of being human. Instead of beating yourself up, see mistakes as learning opportunities. This mindset can boost your confidence. Errors aren't the end of the world!

5. **Body Language:** Your posture and body language can influence how you feel. Standing tall, making eye contact, and smiling can make you feel more confident. It's like a power pose for your self-esteem!

6. **Help Others:** Helping classmates or volunteering can make you feel good and valued and can also boost your self-confidence. It's a win-win!

Building self-confidence takes time, but every step you take makes a difference. Just like leveling up in a game, each small victory adds up to a big boost in your confidence. Keep at it, and you'll be amazed at how strong you can be.

OVERCOMING SELF-DOUBT

Self-doubt is like a sneaky shadow that tries to follow you around, especially during middle school years. But guess what? You have the power to step into the sunlight and leave that shadow behind. Here's how you can overcome self-doubt and shine bright:

1. **Recognize the Doubt:** The first step is to recognize when you're doubting yourself. Are you thinking things like, "I'm not good enough," or, "I can't do this"? Acknowledging these thoughts is the first step to overcoming them.

2. **Challenge Negative Thoughts:** When self-doubt creeps in, challenge it. Ask yourself, "Is this really true?" or "What evidence do I have that contradicts this thought?" Often, you'll find that self-doubt isn't based on facts.

3. **Talk to Someone:** Sometimes, sharing your doubts with a friend, family member, or teacher can help. They can offer a different perspective and remind you of your strengths and abilities.

4. **Focus on What You Can Control:** You might not be able to control everything, but you can control your effort and attitude. Focusing on these can help reduce feelings of self-doubt.

5. **Celebrate Small Successes:** Overcoming self-doubt isn't about making one giant leap; it's about taking small steps. Celebrate your progress, no matter how small, and use it as motivation to keep going.

6. **Practice Self-Compassion:** Be kind to yourself. Remember, everyone experiences self-doubt at times—it doesn't define your worth or abilities.

Overcoming self-doubt is like completing a challenging level in a game. It might take a few tries, but with patience and persistence, you'll get there. And when you do, you'll feel stronger and more confident than ever.

REAL STORIES: DISCOVERING YOUR INNER STRENGTH

The narratives in this section illustrate the journey of overcoming insecurities and embracing self-worth. It highlights the stories of students who have learned to nurture their self-esteem.

STORY 1: EMBRACING IMPERFECTION

Roman, a 6th grader, was always insecure and second-guessing himself. He was the kid who would do everything to please the teacher and his friends, trying not to upset anyone, but it was a burden at times. One day, he made a mistake on his quiz and felt discouraged only to realize that his friends all made the same mistakes regularly and that they cared about him more than his mistake.

STORY 2: SEEKING SUPPORT

Melissa sometimes felt insecure about the fact that she was a bit overweight, and she would withhold some of herself from others afraid that she would be made fun of. But somewhere deep inside, she wondered if it was all in her head and decided to talk to a counselor who met with her regularly to help her accept her strengths and develop skills to face her insecurities.

STORY 3: FINDING LIKE-MINDED PEERS

Lauren was one of the smartest students in the 8th grade, but she struggled to work in groups. She felt like the other students made fun of her because she took the work too seriously. At the quarterly awards ceremony, she realized that many of the students who were making the honor roll and principal's honor roll were in her classes. She realized there were others like her who she could seek out in her classes.

———————————————

These narratives emphasize the value of accepting your flaws, looking for help, and connecting with like-minded peers. By nurturing your self-esteem, you can build a stronger sense of self-worth and confidence.

ACTIVITY 1: CONFIDENCE COLLAGE

Create a collage that represents confidence to you. Use magazine cutouts, drawings, or any other materials. Include images of activities you're good at, people who inspire you, and quotes that boost your confidence. This collage can be a visual reminder of your strengths and aspirations.

REFLECTION 1: OVERCOMING A CHALLENGE

Write about a time when you overcame a challenge. What did you learn about yourself? How did it make you feel? Reflecting on these moments can reinforce your self-belief and resilience.

ACTIVITY 2: THE COMPLIMENT JAR

Start a compliment jar. Whenever someone compliments you, write down the compliment and put it in the jar. When you're feeling down or doubting yourself, read the compliments to remind yourself of your positive qualities and achievements. Using the space below, brainstorm compliments you could give to people you know.

REFLECTION 2: FUTURE DREAMS

Think about what you want to achieve in the future. It could be any-thing from learning a new skill to achieving a personal goal. Write down the steps you can take to reach this goal. Planning for the future can boost your confidence and give you a clear direction.

_____

_____

_____

_____

_____

_____

_____

_____

_____

_____

_____

_____

_____

_____

_____

DOODLE CANVAS: LET YOUR PEN ROAM FREE!

Explore. Experiment. Express.

The focus of this guide is you! You can draw, write, paste your favorite stickers, or record special moments in this space. Make it reflect your individuality!

RESOURCE LIST

- **Inspirational Podcasts and Videos:** Explore online resources for motivational and faith-based content.
- **Counseling and Guidance Services:** Seek guidance from religious leaders, school counselors, or trusted adults for personal and spiritual development.
- **Confidence-Building Workshops:** Look for local workshops or online courses focused on building self-esteem and confidence.
- **Positive Parenting, Thriving Kids:** Provides resources and reviews to help families and educators foster self-esteem in children through positive media and entertainment (https://childmind.org/).

These resources provide support and guidance in helping you to develop your self-esteem. A positive outlook of yourself and how you fit into the context of your school can positively impact your middle school experience.

Chapter 4

Introduction to Exploring Personal Growth

- Brief overview of the concept of personal growth
- Emphasis on the journey of self-improvement and development

Setting Goals and Embracing Challenges

- Discussing how setting goals is vital for personal growth
- Tips on identifying goals and embracing challenges as opportunities

The Importance of Resilience

- Exploring resilience as a key component of personal growth
- Strategies to build and maintain resilience in various situations

Learning from Setbacks

- Understanding that setbacks are part of the growth process
- Techniques for learning and growing from these experiences

Real Stories: Rising Above Adversity

- Anonymized stories from students about conquering difficulties

Activities and Reflections

- Interactive exercises focused on goal-setting and overcoming challenges
- Journal prompts for self-reflection on personal growth experiences

Personalization Space and Resource Directory

- Space for students to document their personal growth journey
- A list of resources for further support in personal development

CHAPTER FOUR

EXPLORING PERSONAL GROWTH

How many times have you stood against a wall for someone to measure your height? Personal growth should happen as naturally as physical growth. This chapter is all about a super important journey—your personal growth. Think of middle school as not just a place where you learn math and science but also where you learn about yourself.

Personal growth is like going on an adventure where you're the hero. It's about setting goals, facing challenges, and becoming the best version of yourself. It's about discovering your strengths, learning from your mistakes, and bouncing back stronger than ever.

In middle school, you'll have plenty of opportunities to grow. You'll face new challenges, like tougher classes, making new friends, or finding your place in different clubs and teams. Each of these experiences is a chance to learn more about who you are and what you're capable of.

But hey, personal growth isn't always a smooth ride. There will be times when you stumble or face obstacles. That's totally okay! It's all part of the process. We'll explore how setting goals can guide you, why being resilient is crucial, and how setbacks can be stepping stones to success.

Get ready to embark on an exciting journey of self-discovery and growth. You're about to learn how to turn challenges into opportunities and setbacks into comebacks!

SETTING GOALS AND EMBRACING CHALLENGES

In middle school, setting goals is like plotting your course on a map. It gives you direction and helps you focus on where you want to go. But it's not just about the destination; it's also about embracing the challenges you'll face along the way.

1. HOW TO SET GOALS

Be Specific: Instead of saying, "I want to do better in school," try, "I want to get a B or higher in math."

Make Them Achievable: Set goals that challenge you but are still attainable.

Write Them Down: Putting your goals on paper makes them more real.

Set Deadlines: This helps you stay on track and motivated.

> Pro tip: Procrastination is the enemy of personal growth. Even if you set goals, procrastination tricks you into thinking you have all the time in the world to achieve them. Without deadlines, there's no need for resilience because you can go at any pace. Plus, there are no setbacks to learn from if you're never pushing yourself to meet a specific timeframe.

2. EMBRACING CHALLENGES

See Challenges as Opportunities: Instead of seeing a tough assignment as a hurdle, view it as a chance to learn something new.

Break Them Down: Big challenges are less daunting when you break them into smaller, manageable tasks.

Stay Positive: Keep a positive attitude. Believe that you can overcome the challenge.

3. CELEBRATING SMALL VICTORIES

Celebrate when you reach a goal or overcome a challenge, to boost your confidence and motivate you for future goals.

Setting goals and embracing challenges are crucial for personal growth. They push you out of your comfort zone and help you discover your potential. Remember, every big achievement starts with the decision to try.

THE IMPORTANCE OF RESILIENCE

Resilience is your superpower in the journey of personal growth. It's the ability to bounce back from setbacks, adapt to change, and keep going in the face of challenges. In middle school, where things are constantly changing, being resilient is key.

1. UNDERSTANDING RESILIENCE

Resilience Is Learnable: It's not just something you're born with—you can develop it.

It Involves Adaptability: Being resilient means being flexible and willing to find new ways to overcome challenges.

2. BUILDING RESILIENCE

Stay Connected: Having a strong support network of friends and family can help you through tough times.

Focus on What You Can Control: You can't control everything that happens, but you can control how you respond.

Take Care of Yourself: Eating well, getting enough sleep, and exercising can boost your mood and energy and make it easier to handle stress.

3. LEARNING FROM SETBACKS

Reflect on Challenges: Think about what you learned from a difficult experience and how it made you stronger.

Stay Optimistic: Keep a positive outlook. Every setback is a chance to grow and improve.

Resilience is about not giving up, even when things get tough. It's about looking at challenges not as insurmountable obstacles, but as opportunities to learn, grow, and become stronger. With resilience, you'll find that you can handle much more than you thought.

LEARNING FROM SETBACKS

Setbacks are not roadblocks; they're stepping stones on your path to personal growth. Learning from them is a crucial part of your middle school journey. Here's how you can turn setbacks into growth opportunities.

1. **Acknowledge Your Feelings:** It's okay to feel disappointed or upset when things don't go as planned. Acknowledge these feelings, but don't let them take over.

2. **Analyze What Happened:** Take a step back and look at the situation. What went wrong? Were there things outside of your control, or are there areas you can improve?

3. **Learn and Adapt:** Every setback has a lesson. Maybe it's about how you study, how you manage your time, or how you handle stress. Identify the lesson and use it to make changes.

4. **Don't Be Too Hard on Yourself:** Remember, everyone faces setbacks. They don't define your worth or your abilities.

5. **Get Back on Track:** Once you've learned from the experience, it's time to move forward. Set new goals and start working toward them.

6. **Seek Support if Needed:** Talking to friends, family, or teachers can provide new perspectives and encouragement.

Learning from setbacks is about resilience, adaptability, and the willingness to keep trying. It's about understanding that growth often comes from challenges and that every experience, good or bad, is a part of your journey to becoming the best version of yourself.

REAL STORIES: RISING ABOVE ADVERSITY

The next three accounts inspire resilience and determination. The following stories recognize students who have faced significant challenges and found ways to overcome them.

STORY 1: PURSUING DREAMS DESPITE HARDSHIPS

Johnny was homeless and forced to live temporarily at a hotel, but he wanted very much to play on the basketball team and enjoy being a kid like everyone else. When tryouts came, he had every reason not to participate, but he opened up about his circumstances to the coach, and after he tried out and made the team, the coach assured him he'd be there to support him through the season.

STORY 2: EXCELLING IN A NEW ENVIRONMENT

Rosa had just arrived from Mexico with her family and knew little to no English. For the first few months, she barely spoke to anyone and often sat by herself or with a handful of other Spanish-speaking students. However, she knew that to succeed, she had to work extra hard at learning English and had to put in the hours outside of school. Despite the challenges she faced in the first year of being here, she excelled in English and her academics, quickly progressing from ESL I to ESL III, and began spending more time with her English-speaking friends than she did with her friends who only spoke Spanish.

STORY 3: MAKING SACRIFICES FOR SUCCESS

Benjamin often had a lot to do at the house when he got home from school because his mom worked late most days. Picking his siblings up from the bus stop, feeding them, and helping them with their homework meant there was little time for him to do his own school work; he knew that he had to choose between going outside for recess or staying in and getting help from his supportive teachers. He decided to stay in from recess. After about a month of doing so, he had caught up on all his missing assignments and was on track to have As and Bs in all his subjects.

Overcoming challenges requires resilience, hard work, and sometimes making sacrifices, as shown by these examples. By facing your difficulties head-on and seeking support, you can achieve your goals and thrive.

ACTIVITY 1: GOAL-SETTING CHART

Create a chart of your goals for the school year. Include short-term and long-term goals, and outline the steps you need to take to achieve them. This chart can be a visual guide and a source of motivation as you work toward your goals.

REFLECTION 1: LEARNING FROM A SETBACK

Think about a time when things didn't go as planned. Write about what happened, how it made you feel, and what you learned from it. Reflecting on this can help you see setbacks as valuable learning experiences.

_____

_____

_____

_____

_____

_____

_____

_____

_____

_____

_____

_____

_____

_____

_____

_____

_____

ACTIVITY 2: RESILIENCE JOURNAL

Start a resilience journal. Whenever you face a challenge, write down how you dealt with it and what you learned. Over time, you'll have a record of your growth and resilience, which can be inspiring to look back on. Using the space below, list some past experiences you could've included in your journal.

-
-
-
-
-
-
-
-
-
-
-

REFLECTION 2: MY SUPPORT SYSTEM

Reflect on the people who support and encourage you. Who are they, and how have they helped you? Recognizing your support system can remind you that you're not alone in your journey of personal growth.

DOODLE CANVAS: LET YOUR PEN ROAM FREE!

Explore. Experiment. Express.

The focus of this guide is you! You can draw, write, paste your favorite stickers, or record special moments in this space. Make it reflect your individuality!

RESOURCE LIST

- **Goal-Setting Apps:** Discover apps to help you set, track, and achieve your goals.
- **Online Learning Platforms:** Access courses and tutorials to learn new skills and hobbies.
- **Youth Groups:** Engage with youth groups in your community for support and guidance.
- **Counseling and Guidance Services:** If you're facing challenges, don't hesitate to reach out to school counselors or local support groups.

These resources provide important information that can support you in your journey of personal growth. As you grow, so too will others around you and the influence you have.

Chapter 5

Introduction to Handling Drama and Conflict

- Brief overview of drama and conflict in middle school
- Emphasis on the importance of healthy conflict resolution

Strategies for Conflict Resolution

- Discussing effective communication techniques for resolving conflicts
- Tips on staying calm and understanding different perspectives

Recognizing Toxic Relationships

- Identifying signs of unhealthy relationships
- Guidance on how to distance oneself from negative influences

Seeking Help When Needed

- Encouraging students to seek support from adults
- Discussing the role of support systems in resolving conflicts and dealing with drama

Real Stories: Turning Conflicts into Connections

- Anonymized stories from students about transforming conflicts into bonds

Activities and Reflections

- Interactive exercises related to conflict resolution and recognizing unhealthy relationships
- Journal prompts to encourage reflection on personal experiences with conflict

Personalization Space and Resource Directory

- Space for students to document their thoughts and experiences regarding conflict
- A list of resources for additional support in conflict resolution and dealing with drama

CHAPTER FIVE

HANDLING DRAMA AND CONFLICT

The typical middle school spans two to three years and is filled with many adventures. Here, we're diving into a crucial part of the middle school experience: handling drama and conflict. Whether it's a disagreement with a friend, a misunderstanding in class, or any other type of conflict, knowing how to handle these situations is an essential skill.

Middle school can sometimes feel like a maze of social interactions, where misunderstandings and conflicts are not uncommon. It's a time when emotions run high and friendships and relationships can be tested. However, it's also a perfect opportunity to develop and strengthen your conflict resolution skills.

We'll explore effective strategies for resolving conflicts, ways to recognize and manage toxic relationships, and the importance of seeking help when needed. You'll learn how to approach and resolve conflicts in a way that is respectful to both yourself and others. We'll also discuss how to maintain your cool in heated situations and how to make decisions that are healthy for you.

Remember, dealing with drama and conflict is part of growing up. It's not about avoiding conflicts altogether but about handling them maturely and constructively. This chapter will equip you with the tools you need to navigate these challenges and emerge stronger and wiser.

So get ready to learn some essential life skills that will help you not just in middle school, but in all walks of life. Let's turn these challenges into opportunities for growth and understanding!

STRATEGIES FOR CONFLICT RESOLUTION

Healthily navigating conflicts is a key skill, not just for middle school but for life. Here are some strategies to help you resolve conflicts effectively:

1. **Stay Calm and Collected:** Take deep breaths and give yourself a moment to cool down before responding. Reacting in anger or frustration often makes things worse.

2. **Listen Actively:** Give the other person your full attention. Listening is more than hearing words; it's about understanding the other person's perspective.

3. **Communicate Clearly:** Use "I" statements to express how you feel without blaming the other person. For example, say "I feel upset when..." instead of "You make me upset because..."

4. **Seek to Understand, Not to Win:** Conflict resolution isn't about winning an argument. It's about understanding each other and finding a solution that works for both sides.

5. **Find Common Ground:** Look for areas of agreement. Starting from a point of agreement can make it easier to work through areas of disagreement.

6. **Agree to Disagree:** Sometimes, you won't see eye to eye, and that's okay. Agreeing to disagree can be a mature way of resolving a conflict.

7. **Know When to Walk Away:** If the conflict escalates or becomes unproductive, it's okay to step back and take a break from the conversation.

8. **Ask for Help if Needed:** If you're struggling to resolve a conflict, it's okay to ask a teacher, counselor, or another trusted adult for help.

Pro tip: One powerful way to resolve drama and conflict is to clearly express how the other person's behavior made you feel. Instead of saying things like, "You lied" or "That's dumb," try saying, "When you said or did that, it really hurt me. I was very disappointed. The trust between us was broken, and that sucks because you're my best friend."

These strategies are about finding respectful and effective ways to handle disagreements and misunderstandings. By applying these techniques, you can turn potentially challenging situations into opportunities for growth and understanding.

RECOGNIZING TOXIC RELATIONSHIPS

Understanding and recognizing toxic relationships is crucial for maintaining your well-being in middle school. A toxic relationship is one that consistently leaves you feeling drained, disrespected, or unhappy. Here's how you can identify and handle these types of relationships:

IDENTIFYING SIGNS OF TOXICITY

Consistent Negativity: If a relationship consistently brings you down or involves a lot of drama, it may be toxic.

Lack of Respect: Disrespectful behavior, like mocking, bullying, or ignoring your feelings, is a red flag.

Control Issues: If a friend tries to control what you do, who you talk to, or how you act, that's not healthy.

One-Sidedness: A relationship should be a two-way street. If you're always giving and never receiving, it might be toxic.

HANDLING TOXIC RELATIONSHIPS

Set Boundaries: Be clear about what behavior you will and will not tolerate.

Speak Up: If you feel safe, express how the person's behavior affects you.

Seek Support: Talk to a trusted adult, like a teacher or counselor, for guidance.

Distance Yourself: Sometimes, the healthiest option is to distance yourself from the toxic relationship.

PRIORITIZING YOUR WELL-BEING

Remember, it's important to prioritize your own mental and emotional health. Surrounding yourself with positive, supportive people is key to your well-being.

Recognizing toxic relationships and understanding how to handle them can help you create a healthier, happier middle school experience. It's about knowing your worth and choosing to spend time with people who respect and support you.

SEEKING HELP WHEN NEEDED

Sometimes, handling drama and conflict on your own can be tough, and that's perfectly normal. Knowing when and how to seek help is a sign of strength and maturity during those challenging times.

RECOGNIZE WHEN TO SEEK HELP

If you're feeling overwhelmed, stressed, or unsafe because of a conflict, it's time to seek help. Persistent problems that don't seem to improve, despite your efforts, also warrant outside assistance.

SOURCES OF HELP:

Trusted Adults: This can be a teacher, school counselor, coach, or family member. They can offer guidance and support and sometimes intervene if necessary.

Peer Mediation: Some schools have peer mediation programs where trained students help others resolve conflicts.

Professional Help: In certain situations, speaking to a mental health professional can be beneficial.

HOW TO ASK FOR HELP

Be honest and clear about the situation and your feelings. Explain why you think you need help. Remember, asking for help isn't a sign of weakness; it's a smart way to handle situations that are beyond your experience or control.

UTILIZE SCHOOL RESOURCES

Many schools offer resources for conflict resolution, such as counseling services or conflict resolution workshops. Take advantage of these resources.

Seeking help when faced with drama and conflict shows that you're responsible and proactive about finding solutions. It's an important part of maintaining your mental and emotional health and ensuring a positive middle school experience.

REAL STORIES: TURNING CONFLICTS INTO CONNECTIONS

This section explores stories of students who have navigated conflicts and found ways to resolve them. These examples highlight the importance of communication and compromise.

STORY 1: MEDIATING FRIENDSHIPS

Jasmine and Kila, to the outside observer, were frenemies because one day they were besties but the next day behaved like they hated each other. Jasmine wanted mediation with the assistant principal but Kila preferred someone from their friend group. Eventually, they compromised and went with the grade-level counselor, and after a few meetings, they no longer looked like frenemies, but BFFs.

STORY 2: ACCEPTING NEW DYNAMICS

Jose and Josh were used to cracking jokes at each other's expense; Josh, however, participated less and less and was more on the receiving end of Jose's jokes. He shared his feelings many times only to be made fun of by Jose. Josh slowly pulled away. He sat with new friends at the lunch table, played with different students at recess, and barely spoke to Jose. After a few weeks, they barely acknowledged each other, but both seemed happy with this new status; that is, not friends anymore.

STORY 3: CONFRONTING RUMORS

Carlene, Sophia, Sierra, and Colleen were close friends who spent a lot of time together in and out of school. At a carnival over the weekend, a rumor started that Carlene was talking badly about the other friends in the group. The rumor spread like wildfire. Before it could be verified or contained, the three girls stopped talking to Carlene; she was devastated and struggled for a couple of days as her friends doubled down on their attitude towards her. When the counselor got involved, the girls were forced to confront the rumor only to realize it was a lie started by another student to break up their friendship. They hugged and made up that day.

Resolving conflicts involves communication, understanding, and sometimes seeking mediation, as observed in these student stories. By addressing issues head-on and working towards a resolution, you can maintain healthy relationships and grow from the experience.

ACTIVITIES AND REFLECTIONS

ACTIVITY 1: CONFLICT RESOLUTION ROLE-PLAY

Pair up with a friend or family member to role-play a conflict situation. Practice using the conflict resolution strategies you've learned, like active listening and using "I" statements. This can help you feel more prepared for real-life situations. In the space below, illustrate potential conflict situations you could role-play.

REFLECTION 1: ANALYZING A PAST CONFLICT

Think of a past conflict you had. Write about what happened, how you handled it, and what you could have done differently. Reflecting on past experiences can help you improve your conflict resolution skills for the future.

_____

_____

_____

_____

_____

_____

_____

_____

_____

_____

_____

_____

_____

_____

ACTIVITY 2: IDENTIFYING TOXIC TRAITS

Create a list of traits that you would consider toxic in a relationship. Next to each trait, write down ways you can address or avoid these behaviors in others. This activity helps you become more aware of what healthy and unhealthy relationships look like.

-
-
-
-
-
-
-
-
-
-
-
-
-
-
-

REFLECTION 2: SEEKING HELP

Reflect on a time when you needed help but hesitated to ask for it. What held you back? How can you overcome these barriers in the future? Recognizing these moments can empower you to seek help when needed.

_____

_____

_____

_____

_____

_____

_____

_____

_____

_____

_____

_____

_____

_____

_____

DOODLE CANVAS: LET YOUR PEN ROAM FREE!

Explore. Experiment. Express.

The focus of this guide is you! You can draw, write, paste your favorite stickers, or record special moments in this space. Make it reflect your individuality!

RESOURCE LIST

- **National Conflict Resolution Center (NCRC):** Offers resources and training on conflict resolution (www.ncrconline. com).
- **Teens Against Bullying:** A platform for teen education and bullying prevention (www.pacerteensagainstbullying.org).
- **StopBullying.gov:** Provides information from various government agencies on how kids, teens, and young adults can prevent or stop bullying (www.stopbullying.gov).
- **Kids Helpline:** A confidential counseling service for young people (1-800-668-6868).

These resources can be very helpful when drama and conflict find you. They are part of the middle school experience. The best strategy to combat them is to focus on your schoolwork and to seek help when needed.

Chapter 6

Introduction to the World of Dating

- Overview of navigating crushes and first relationships in middle school
- Emphasis on the emotional aspects and the importance of maturity

Navigating Crushes and First Relationships

- Discussing the feelings and experiences associated with having a crush
- Tips for starting and maintaining a healthy first relationship

Understanding Consent and Boundaries

- Explaining the concept of consent in relationships
- Importance of setting and respecting personal boundaries

Coping with Heartbreak

- Strategies for dealing with the end of a relationship
- Emphasis on self-care and emotional well-being

Real Stories: Balancing Friendships and Your Enmeshment

- Anonymized stories from students about managing relationships and maintaining individuality

Activities and Reflections

- Interactive exercises related to understanding relationships
- Journal prompts to encourage self-reflection on personal experiences with dating

Personalization Space and Resource Directory

- Space for students to document their thoughts and experiences related to dating
- A list of nationally known resources for additional support in the realm of young relationships

CHAPTER SIX

THE WORLD OF DATING

As a youth growing up in Trinidad and Tobago, whenever someone mentioned that a middle school kid was dating, the typical parent's response would be, "Stop studying boys/girls and study your books!" In this chapter, we're entering the world of dating—a topic that can be exciting, confusing, and a little nerve-wracking, all at the same time.

Middle school often marks the beginning of new feelings—like having crushes and maybe even starting your first relationship. These experiences are a normal part of growing up, but they come with their own set of questions and emotions. How do you tell someone you like them? What does it mean to be in a relationship at this age? How do you handle the ups and downs that come with these feelings?

We'll explore how to navigate these new experiences healthily and respectfully. You'll learn about the importance of understanding and giving consent, setting personal boundaries, and the value of mutual respect in relationships. Remember, every relationship, whether it lasts or not, is a chance to learn more about yourself and how you relate to others.

And what about when things don't work out? We'll also talk about coping with heartbreak and the importance of taking care of yourself emotionally.

Let's dive into the world of dating and get equipped with the knowledge and skills to handle your first crushes and relationships positively and maturely.

NAVIGATING CRUSHES AND FIRST RELATIONSHIPS

Middle school is often where the journey into the world of crushes and first relationships begins. It's a time filled with new emotions and experiences that can be both thrilling and overwhelming.

UNDERSTANDING CRUSHES

A crush is a sudden rush of affection towards someone. It's normal to feel nervous or excited around your crush.

Remember, it's okay if your feelings aren't reciprocated. Crushes are a natural part of growing up and learning about romantic feelings.

STARTING A RELATIONSHIP

- **Communication is Key:** If you're interested in someone, it's okay to express your feelings, but always respect their response, whether it's positive or not.
- **Healthy Relationships:** A good relationship is based on mutual respect, honesty, and enjoying spending time together. It should feel supportive, not stressful.

RESPECT AND BOUNDARIES

Every person has the right to set their boundaries. It's important to communicate and respect each other's comfort levels in a relationship.

PEER PRESSURE

Don't feel pressured to be in a relationship just because others are. It's perfectly fine to wait until you're ready.

ENJOYING THE EXPERIENCE

Relationships at this age should be about getting to know each other and having fun. It's not about seriousness but about learning how to interact with someone you like.

Navigating crushes and first relationships is a significant step in your growth journey. It's about understanding your feelings, respecting others, and enjoying this new phase of life responsibly.

UNDERSTANDING CONSENT AND BOUNDARIES

Understanding consent and setting boundaries are crucial aspects of any relationship, especially in middle school.

WHAT IS CONSENT?

Consent is a clear and enthusiastic agreement to engage in any form of interaction, be it hanging out, holding hands, or staying on the phone for hours.

It's important to understand that consent should always be given freely, without any pressure or coercion.

SETTING BOUNDARIES

Personal boundaries vary from person to person. It's important to communicate your boundaries clearly and also ask and respect others' boundaries.

Remember, it's okay to say no at any time, and it's important to respect a 'no' from others as well.

OPEN COMMUNICATION

Having open and honest conversations about feelings, boundaries, and consent is key to a healthy and respectful relationship.

RECOGNIZING UNHEALTHY BEHAVIORS

If someone doesn't respect your boundaries or makes you feel uncomfortable, it's a red flag. Trust your feelings and seek help from a trusted adult if needed.

Understanding and practicing consent and respecting boundaries are essential for building safe and healthy relationships. It's about mutual respect and caring for each other's well-being.

COPING WITH HEARTBREAK

Heartbreak, although painful, is a part of life and learning about relationships. It's especially challenging during the sensitive years of middle school. Here's how to navigate and cope with the end of a relationship:

1. **Allow Yourself to Feel:** It's okay to feel sad, disappointed, or even angry. Allow yourself to experience these emotions without judgment.

2. **Talk About It:** Share your feelings with a trusted friend, family member, or counselor. Talking about what you're going through can be very therapeutic.

3. **Stay Active and Engaged:** Keep up with your hobbies, sports, and other activities. Staying busy can help take your mind off the heartbreak and remind you of the other enjoyable aspects of life.

4. **Avoid Dwelling on Negativity:** While it's important to acknowledge your feelings, try not to get stuck in negative thoughts. Remember, this experience will not define your future relationships.

5. **Learn from the Experience:** Reflect on what you've learned from the relationship and the breakup. Each experience, no matter how painful, contributes to your growth and understanding of yourself.

6. **Give Yourself Time:** Healing takes time. Be patient with yourself and don't rush into another relationship until you're ready.

Coping with heartbreak is about acknowledging your feelings, learning from the experience, and gradually moving forward. Remember, it's a part of growing up, and with time, you will feel better.

> Pro tip: If you can avoid getting entangled in a relationship, it is ultimately better for an enriching middle school experience. The tips outlined here are general suggestions for those of you already dating or interested in someone. However, relationships at this age and grade (even good ones), often come with a heavy price that includes a loss of great friends, an unfulfilling middle school experience, and great sadness and depression. Ultimately, I have found that students who are fully engaged in the learning activities at school; that is, their academics, clubs, sports, and having healthy friendships are almost always happy and enjoy coming to school.

REAL STORIES: BALANCING FRIENDSHIPS AND YOUR ENMESHMENT

The Real Stories of Chapter 6 give a sneak-peek into how some students have managed the complexities of relationships. Their experiences provide insights into the challenges and lessons learned from dating during middle school.

STORY 1: BALANCING RELATIONSHIPS AND FRIENDSHIPS

Tyler and Nyosa started dating at the end of 7th grade. The first few months of their relationship were quite rocky, and they often went to school looking depressed and unhappy. That changed within a few months; they spent less time with each other, but were still dating and were generally happier. One time they went to Six Flags but spent most of their time with their individual friends. When pressed about whether or not they were still dating, they both said "yes" but they learned how to maintain their other friendships and still be okay.

STORY 2: HANDLING DISRUPTIVE RELATIONSHIPS

When Jaylen and Rihanna started dating, it was quite a surprise to everyone because they were so different. And from the very beginning of their relationship, they began to misbehave at school. They were often late for class, messing around at their lockers, leaving and cutting classes to see each other, and constantly causing a disruption. When they eventually broke up, Rihanna remarked, "I can't believe I fought a girl for him..."

STORY 3: KNOWING YOUR LIMITS

John had no real intentions of dating but when Jasmine, the new girl, arrived, everyone encouraged him to talk to her because it was rumored that she liked him; so he reluctantly did. They went out to the "movies" a few times and spent a lot of time talking on the phone but then John abruptly ended it because he felt that Jasmine was moving too fast and wanted to do things that he was not ready to do.

Navigating relationships in middle school can be challenging and may come with significant consequences, as demonstrated by these students. By maintaining balance, setting boundaries, and knowing your limits, you can manage relationships in a way that supports your overall well-being and happiness.

ACTIVITIES AND REFLECTIONS

ACTIVITY 1: MY FEELINGS JOURNAL

Start a journal to express your feelings about crushes, relationships, and any heartbreak. Writing can help you process your emotions and gain clarity. Using the space below, list some feelings, experiences, or situations you could include in your journal.

-
-
-
-
-
-
-
-
-
-

REFLECTION 1: RELATIONSHIP REFLECTIONS

Reflect on what qualities you value in a relationship. What have you learned about yourself from your experiences with crushes and relationships?

_____

_____

_____

_____

_____

_____

_____

_____

_____

_____

_____

_____

_____

_____

_____

ACTIVITY 2: LETTER TO MY FUTURE SELF

Write a letter to your future self about your current experiences with dating, your feelings, and what you hope to learn. This can be a meaningful way to see how much you've grown when you read it in the future.

_____

_____

_____

_____

_____

_____

_____

_____

_____

_____

_____

_____

_____

_____

REFLECTION 2: LEARNING FROM HEARTBREAK

Think about a time you experienced disappointment or heartbreak. What did it teach you? How did it contribute to your growth?

_____

_____

_____

_____

_____

_____

_____

_____

_____

_____

_____

_____

_____

_____

_____

_____

_____

DOODLE CANVAS: LET YOUR PEN ROAM FREE!

Explore. Experiment. Express.

The focus of this guide is you! You can draw, write, paste your favorite stickers, or record special moments in this space. Make it reflect your individuality!

RESOURCE LIST

- **Kids Helpline:** A confidential counseling service for young people (1-800-668-6868).
- **Teen Line:** A confidential hotline for teen-to-teen advice and support (www.teenlineonline.org).
- **Kids Health:** https://kidshealth.org/

These nationally recognized resources offer support and guidance in the realm of young relationships. They can help you navigate the complexities of dating, consent, and emotional well-being.

Chapter 7

Introduction to Balancing Academics and Fun

- Overview of the challenge of balancing schoolwork and social activities
- The importance of a balanced lifestyle in middle school

Time Management Tips

- Practical advice on how to manage time effectively
- Strategies for organizing schoolwork and extracurricular activities

Finding a Balance Between School and Social Life

- Tips on maintaining a healthy social life while keeping up with academics
- Importance of taking breaks and making time for fun

Setting Priorities

- Guidance on how to prioritize tasks and activities
- The role of setting goals in balancing different aspects of life

Real Stories: Mastering the Juggle

- Anonymized stories from students about achieving a balance between school and activities

Activities and Reflections

- Interactive exercises related to time management and setting priorities
- Journal prompts to encourage reflection on balancing academics and social life

Personalization Space and Resource Directory

- Space for students to document their strategies for balancing school and fun
- A list of resources providing additional tips and tools for effective time management and balance

CHAPTER SEVEN

BALANCING ACADEMICS AND FUN

Middle school is filled with many gifted and talented students, scholar-athletes, and hard-working students who just want to enjoy the experience. The following pages tackle a crucial aspect of your middle school journey—finding the right balance between academics and fun.

Middle school brings a new level of academic responsibility. There are more subjects, homework, and projects. At the same time, your social life becomes more vibrant. There are after-school activities, sports, hobbies, and time with friends. Juggling all these can feel like a tightrope walk, but with the right strategies, you can maintain a healthy balance.

Achieving this balance is essential not only for your academic success but also for your overall well-being. It's about managing your time effectively, setting the right priorities, and still making room for fun and relaxation. This chapter will provide you with practical time management tips, ways to find harmony between schoolwork and social activities, and guidance on setting your priorities.

Remember, balancing academics and fun is about making smart choices and planning. It's about understanding that both aspects are important for your growth and happiness. Let's explore how you can master this balancing act and make the most of your middle school years.

TIME MANAGEMENT TIPS

Mastering time management is a superpower that can transform your middle school experience. Here are some tips to help you manage your time wisely:

- **Use a Planner or Calendar:** Keep track of assignments, tests, and extracurricular activities. Seeing everything in one place can help you plan your time better.
- **Break Tasks into Smaller Steps:** Large assignments can feel

overwhelming. Break them into smaller, manageable tasks and tackle them one at a time.

- **Set Specific Times for Studying:** Designate specific times for homework and studying each day. Having a routine can improve focus and efficiency.
- **Prioritize Tasks:** Determine which tasks are most urgent and important. Tackle these first to ensure you're meeting key deadlines.
- **Avoid Procrastination:** Try to start on assignments as soon as they're given. Waiting until the last minute can lead to unnecessary stress. See Pro Tip in Chapter 4.
- **Take Regular Breaks:** Taking short breaks during study sessions can boost your concentration and prevent burnout.
- **Limit Distractions:** Find a quiet place to study and keep distractions like TV and social media to a minimum.
- **Balance School and Leisure:** Make sure to schedule time for relaxation and fun. All work and no play makes Jack a dull boy; trust me, I know all about Jack—get it, Dr. Jack, the author of this book... nvm!

Effective time management is about making the most of your available time, which allows you to excel in academics while still enjoying your middle school life.

FINDING A BALANCE BETWEEN SCHOOL AND SOCIAL LIFE

Balancing your schoolwork with your social life is like finding the perfect mix of ingredients in a recipe—it takes trial and error, but the result is worth it.

Understand Your Limits: Recognize that there are only so many hours in a day. Be realistic about what you can accomplish and still have time for fun.

Make Time for Friends and Interests: Schedule time for hanging out with friends, hobbies, and relaxation, just like you would for homework and studying.

Communicate with Family and Friends: Let your family and friends know about your busy times, like exam weeks, so they understand when you might be less available.

Stay Flexible: Sometimes, unexpected things come up. Be ready to adjust your schedule as needed.

—————————

Finding a balance is crucial for your mental and emotional well-being. It allows you to enjoy the best of both worlds—succeeding in school and having a fulfilling social life.

SETTING PRIORITIES

Setting priorities is like being the captain of your own ship; you decide the course based on what's most important. Here's how to effectively set priorities in your middle school life:

1. **Identify What's Most Important:** Take a moment to think about what's most important to you—both academically and personally. This could be excelling in a particular subject, spending time on a hobby, or being with friends.

2. **Make a To-Do List:** Write down everything you need to do, both for school and in your personal life. Seeing it all on paper (or a screen) can help you figure out what to tackle first.

3. **Categorize Tasks:** Divide your tasks into categories like

'urgent,' 'important,' and 'can wait.' This helps in focusing on what needs immediate attention.

4. **Be Realistic:** Understand your capabilities and limits. Don't overload yourself with too many commitments.

5. **Review and Adjust Regularly:** Your priorities might change, and that's okay. Regularly review and adjust them as needed.

6. **Learn to Say No:** Sometimes, you might have to turn down social invitations or extra activities to focus on your priorities. Learning to maintain balance is an important skill to develop.

By setting priorities, you take control of how you spend your time and energy. It helps in focusing on what truly matters to you and can lead to a more fulfilling and balanced middle school experience.

Pro tip: Watch out for peer pressure and friends with different goals. They might not want the same things as you or might spend their time differently, and that's perfectly fine. Recognize this early on and take steps to make sure you don't compromise your own priorities and goals because of them.

REAL STORIES: MASTERING THE JUGGLE

In this part, we're focusing on how students juggle school work and extracurricular activities. These stories show the importance of time management and finding balance between academics and hobbies.

STORY 1: PRIORITIZING ACTIVITIES

Jiang started 6th grade at a private school where he only played basketball and took karate classes. In 7th grade he attended a traditional middle school and became interested in track and field and chess. He now had three important extra-curricular activities he was good at and enjoyed in addition to attending youth group at his church on Wednesdays. Jiang knew that he could not participate in all those activities, so he prioritized based on what was most important and decided to only play chess online, and to only do track in the spring.

STORY 2: STAYING ON TOP OF ACADEMICS

Emma was very good at basketball but struggled to keep her grades up during the basketball season. She knew that if she failed any of her classes she'd go on academic probation and not be able to play. Emma decided to pay a lot more attention in class, asked the teacher and her friends for help with anything she didn't understand, and made sure she did her school work first when she got home from practice and games before getting on social media.

STORY 3: SETTING PERSONAL GOALS

Wesley knew that he needed more time to process information and to complete tasks. His teachers had done a very good job of making the necessary accommodations for him in class, but Wesley had to follow through on his end. With the help of his counselor and parents, Wesley set an alarm on his phone to begin his homework every night, and an alarm to take breaks. He was now able to be successful on his own.

Jiang, Emma, and Wesley show us that balancing academics and extracurricular activities requires prioritization and time management. By setting goals and making smart choices, you can excel in both areas and enjoy a well-rounded middle school experience.

ACTIVITY 1: PRIORITY MATRIX

Create a matrix to categorize your weekly tasks. Use four quadrants: Urgent and Important, Important but Not Urgent, Urgent but Not Important, and Neither Urgent nor Important. This can help you visualize and prioritize your weekly tasks.

	URGENT	**NOT URGENT**
IMPORTANT		
NOT IMPORTANT		

REFLECTION 1: BALANCING ACT

Reflect on a week when you felt both academically successful and socially fulfilled. What did you do differently? How can you apply those strategies to other weeks?

_____

_____

_____

_____

_____

_____

_____

_____

_____

_____

_____

_____

_____

_____

_____

_____

_____

_____

ACTIVITY 2: TIME AUDIT

Keep a diary for a week and note how you spend your time each day. Review it to see where you might be able to manage your time better. What did you discover about your time management?

_____

_____

_____

_____

_____

_____

_____

_____

_____

_____

_____

_____

_____

_____

_____

REFLECTION 2: SAYING NO

Think of a time you said yes to something but later wished you had said no. Reflect on why you said yes and how you can be more assertive about your priorities in the future.

_____

_____

_____

_____

_____

_____

_____

_____

_____

_____

_____

_____

_____

_____

_____

_____

_____

DOODLE CANVAS: LET YOUR PEN ROAM FREE!

Explore. Experiment. Express.

The focus of this guide is you! You can draw, write, paste your favorite stickers, or record special moments in this space. Make it reflect your individuality!

RESOURCE LIST

- **My Study Life (App):** A cross-platform planner for students to manage their time effectively (www.mystudylife.com).
- **Time Management for Teens (Book):** Provides practical tips and strategies specifically for teenagers.
- **Mindfulness for Teens (Website):** Offers resources and exercises to help teens stay focused and balanced (www. mindfulnessforteens.com).
- **Khan Academy (Educational Resource):** Free online courses for extra academic support (www.khanacademy.org).

These resources offer valuable tools and information to help you manage your time effectively and maintain a healthy balance between academics and social activities.

Chapter 8

Introduction to Coping with Stress and Anxiety

- Overview of common stressors in middle school
- Emphasizing the normalcy of feeling stressed or anxious and the importance of addressing these feelings

Recognizing Stressors in Middle School

- Identifying common sources of stress for middle school students
- Discussion on the signs of stress and anxiety

Developing Coping Mechanisms

- Strategies for managing stress, such as relaxation techniques and healthy habits
- Tips on building resilience and dealing with anxiety

The Importance of Self-Care

- Explaining how self-care practices contribute to stress reduction
- Ideas for self-care activities and routines

Real Stories: Finding Balance in the Day to Day

- Anonymized stories from students about maintaining equilibrium in daily life

Activities and Reflections

- Interactive exercises and journaling prompts focused on recognizing stress and developing coping strategies

Personalization Space and Resource Directory

- Space for students to note their coping strategies and reflections on stress management
- A list of resources providing additional support and information on coping with stress and anxiety

CHAPTER EIGHT

COPING WITH STRESS AND ANXIETY

How do you become more resilient and less worried and stressed by the many things you are facing at this age? In this chapter, we delve into an important topic that affects many middle school students: coping with stress and anxiety.

Middle school is a time of significant changes—new academic responsibilities, evolving social dynamics, and personal growth. It's completely normal to feel stressed or anxious at times. Whether it's worrying about grades, navigating friendships, or dealing with other pressures, understanding how to manage these feelings is crucial.

We'll explore the common stressors you might face in middle school and learn how to recognize the signs of stress and anxiety. It's important to remember that you're not alone in feeling this way, and there are many ways to manage these emotions effectively.

This section will guide you through developing healthy coping mechanisms, the importance of self-care, and how to maintain your mental and emotional well-being. By learning these skills, you can become more resilient and better equipped to handle the challenges of middle school and beyond.

Let's start this journey towards understanding and managing stress and anxiety and ensure you have the tools you need for a more balanced and enjoyable middle school experience.

RECOGNIZING STRESSORS IN MIDDLE SCHOOL

Identifying what causes stress and anxiety is the first step toward managing them effectively. Middle school brings a mix of challenges that can be significant stressors:

1. **Academic Pressure:** Increased workload, higher expectations,

and preparing for high school can cause stress. Worries about grades and performance are common.

2. **Social Changes:** Navigating friendships, peer pressure, and wanting to fit in can be stressful. Social dynamics in middle school are often complex and ever-changing.

3. **Personal Growth:** The physical and emotional changes during adolescence can contribute to stress and anxiety. Concerns about self-image and identity are prevalent.

4. **Signs of Stress and Anxiety:**
   - Physical signs, like headaches, stomachaches, or tiredness.
   - Emotional signs, like irritability, mood swings, or feeling overwhelmed.
   - Behavioral changes, like withdrawing from activities or changes in eating or sleeping habits.

Recognizing these stressors and signs is the first step in managing them. It's important to understand that experiencing stress and anxiety is normal and there are ways to cope effectively.

DEVELOPING COPING MECHANISMS

Developing healthy coping mechanisms is essential for managing stress and anxiety. Here are some strategies that can help:

- **Relaxation Techniques:** Certain practices, like deep breathing, meditation, or yoga can help calm your mind and reduce stress.
- **Time Management:** Organizing your schedule and setting priorities can help manage academic pressures.
- **Healthy Habits:** Regular exercise, a balanced diet, and adequate sleep are crucial for stress reduction.

- **Talking About It:** Sharing your feelings with a trusted adult, friend, or counselor can provide relief and perspective.
- **Mindfulness and Positive Thinking:** Focusing on the present and maintaining a positive outlook can reduce anxiety about the future.
- **Hobbies and Interests:** Engaging in activities you enjoy can be a great stress reliever.

Implementing these coping mechanisms can help you manage stress and anxiety, which can make your middle school years more enjoyable and less overwhelming.

THE IMPORTANCE OF SELF-CARE

Self-care is about taking the time to look after your physical, emotional, spiritual, and mental well-being. It plays a crucial role in managing stress and anxiety:

- **Understanding Self-Care:** Self-care is any activity that you do deliberately to take care of your mental, emotional, and physical health.
- **Simple Self-Care Practices:** Activities like reading, listening to music, or spending time in nature can be soothing. Maintaining a routine that includes time for relaxation and fun is key.
- **Balancing Social Time and Alone Time:** While socializing is important, having some quiet time for yourself is also essential for recharging.
- **Seeking Professional Help When Needed:** Sometimes, talking to a mental health professional can be a vital part of self-care.

Practicing self-care is not selfish; it's necessary for your overall well-being and effectiveness in dealing with life's challenges.

> Pro tip: Be careful not to spend too much time on social media. Even when you intend to just casually browse, ads and other stress-inducing reels can pop up, stealing your joy, peace, and positive thoughts.

REAL STORIES: FINDING BALANCE IN THE DAY TO DAY

How can you effectively manage the stress and anxiety that come with being a middle school student? The following student narratives show that, with the right strategies and support, you can overcome these challenges.

STORY 1: DISCOVERING JOY IN NEW ROUTINES

Latisha was in a four hour detention and announced to the teacher supervising how much she enjoyed her time reading and talking to her. The teacher relished the time with her, but, surprised by her statement, asked her about her routine at home. Latisha stated that when she gets home, after saying "hi" to her family, she goes to her room and spends time on her phone or social media for the rest of the evening. "I've learned so much and really enjoyed the past four hours of reading and talking to you that I want to do it again."

STORY 2: COPING WITH CROWDED SPACES

Casey struggles with crowded spaces, so her anxiety is sky-high at the start of the day when students are packed into the halls going to their classes, at transitions when a period ends, and at the end of recess when everyone is reentering the building from playing outside. To cope with this reality, Casey spoke to her counselor who informed her teachers and got permission for her to either head to her classes earlier, wait for the halls to clear before she transitions, or to use a separate entrance into the building at the end of recess.

STORY 3: FINDING FAMILY SUPPORT

Elvis and his family usually sit together at the dining table and discuss their day during dinner. Everyone is expected to share. Elvis loves his family and values their opinion. After saying grace, he gladly tells about some of the challenges he faces and eagerly listens to the advice of his parents and older brother, who he looks up to. Before going to bed, he says his prayers and writes down his thoughts and the advice he got in his personal journal. In the morning, he quickly reads what he wrote the night prior, before heading out to catch the bus.

Managing stress and anxiety is possible with the right routines, support systems, and coping strategies. These students used their teachers, counselors, and family to help them. It's important to find what works best for you and seek help when needed.

ACTIVITY 1: STRESS DIARY

Keep a diary for a week and note when you feel stressed or anxious and what triggered these feelings. At the end of the week, review your diary to identify patterns and possible solutions. What did you notice?

_____

_____

_____

_____

_____

_____

_____

_____

_____

_____

_____

_____

_____

_____

_____

REFLECTION 1: MY RELAXATION TECHNIQUES

Reflect on what activities help you relax and feel calm. How can you incorporate these activities into your daily or weekly routine?

_____

_____

_____

_____

_____

_____

_____

_____

_____

_____

_____

_____

_____

_____

_____

_____

ACTIVITY 2: TIME MANAGEMENT PLAN

Create a weekly schedule that balances schoolwork, hobbies, social time, and relaxation. This plan can help you manage your time more effectively and reduce stress.

SUNDAY

MONDAY

TUESDAY

WEDNESDAY

THURSDAY

FRIDAY

SATURDAY

REFLECTION 2: LEARNING FROM STRESS

Think about a stressful situation you managed well. What did you learn from that experience? How can you apply those lessons to future stressors?

_____

_____

_____

_____

_____

_____

_____

_____

_____

_____

_____

_____

_____

_____

_____

_____

_____

DOODLE CANVAS: LET YOUR PEN ROAM FREE!

Explore. Experiment. Express.

The focus of this guide is you! You can draw, write, paste your favorite stickers, or record special moments in this space. Make it reflect your individuality!

RESOURCE LIST

- **American Psychological Association (APA):** Offers resources on managing stress (www.apa.org).
- **Mindfulness for Teens:** Provides tools and practices for mindfulness and stress reduction (www.mindfulnessforteens. com).
- **Teen Mental Health:** A resource for understanding and improving teen mental health (www.teenmentalhealth.org).
- **National Alliance on Mental Illness (NAMI):** Offers support and education for young people dealing with mental health issues (www.nami.org).

These resources provide additional support and information to help you cope with stress and anxiety and promote a healthy approach to managing your mental and emotional well-being.

Chapter 9

Introduction to Preparing for High School

- Overview of the transition from middle to high school
- Emphasizing the new opportunities and challenges

Setting Academic and Personal Goals

- Guidance on how to set effective goals for high school
- Discussing the importance of both academic and personal goal-setting

Advice for Success in High School

- Sharing tips and strategies for thriving academically, socially, and personally in high school
- Emphasizing the skills needed for high school success

Understanding High School Expectations

- Outlining the typical academic and social expectations in high school
- Preparing for the increased responsibilities and independence

Real Stories: Preparing for the Next Big Step

- Anonymized stories from students about getting ready for high school

Activities and Reflections

- Interactive exercises and journaling prompts focused on preparing for high school

Personalization Space and Resource Directory

- Space for students to note their goals and plans for high school
- A list of resources providing additional support and information for high school preparation

CHAPTER NINE

PREPARING FOR HIGH SCHOOL

As you approach the end of your middle school journey, an exciting new chapter awaits: high school. This transition is a significant milestone and marks the beginning of new challenges, opportunities, and experiences. Now is as good a time as any to begin thinking about it.

High school is a time for greater academic challenges, more diverse extracurricular options, and new social dynamics. It's a time of significant personal growth, where you'll have more independence and the chance to explore your interests more deeply.

This chapter will guide you through the process of preparing for high school. We'll discuss how to set effective academic and personal goals, get some advice for success, and learn what to expect when you step into this new phase of your education. You'll learn how to navigate the transition smoothly and make the most of the opportunities that high school offers.

The move to high school is a big step, but with the right preparation and mindset, it can be an incredibly rewarding experience. Let's get ready to make this transition with confidence and excitement!

SETTING ACADEMIC AND PERSONAL GOALS

Setting clear academic and personal goals is crucial as you prepare to enter high school. These goals will serve as your roadmap and will guide you through the new experiences and challenges you'll face.

ACADEMIC GOALS

Focus on Your Interests: High school offers a wider range of subjects. Think about what interests you and how you can pursue those subjects.

Plan for College or a Career: Start thinking about your long-term academic goals, like college or a specific career path. Consider what classes or activities might help you prepare.

Pro tip: Your counselor is one of the most important people to talk to at this time.

Improve Study Habits: High school work is more demanding. Set goals to develop stronger study habits that will help you succeed.

PERSONAL GOALS

Developing New Skills: Whether it's learning a new language, an instrument, or a sport, high school is a great time to explore and develop new skills.

Building Relationships: Set goals to expand your social circle, make new friends, and develop meaningful relationships.

Personal Growth: Consider goals related to personal development, like becoming more organized, improving your time management skills, or cultivating leadership qualities.

SETTING SMART GOALS

Ensure your goals are Specific, Measurable, Achievable, Relevant, and Time-bound. SMART goals provide clarity and a deadline for achievement.

REVIEW AND ADJUST

Regularly review your goals to track your progress. Be flexible and adjust them as needed based on your experiences and changing interests.

Setting both academic and personal goals helps you stay focused and motivated, which ensures a well-rounded and fulfilling high school experience.

ADVICE FOR SUCCESS IN HIGH SCHOOL

Transitioning to high school can be overwhelming, but with the right approach, you can thrive both academically and personally. Here are some key pieces of advice for success in high school:

- **Stay Organized:** High school comes with more responsibilities. Staying organized can help you manage your coursework and activities efficiently.
- **Get Involved:** Participate in clubs, sports, or arts that interest you. These activities are not only enjoyable but also opportunities for learning and personal growth.
- **Build Strong Relationships:** Develop positive relationships with your teachers and peers. These connections can be supportive and beneficial throughout your high school years.
- **Seek Help When Needed:** Don't hesitate to ask for help. Teachers and school counselors are there to support you in your academic and personal challenges.
- **Take Care of Yourself:** Pay attention to your physical and mental health. Balance your studies with time for relaxation and activities you enjoy.
- **Embrace New Experiences:** High school is a time to explore new interests and challenge yourself. Be open to new experiences and learning opportunities.

Pro tip: Try to resist the temptation to follow your friends; instead chart your own path based on your interests.

Following these tips can help you make the most of your high school years and allow you to set a strong foundation for your future.

UNDERSTANDING HIGH SCHOOL EXPECTATIONS

Transitioning to high school comes with a set of expectations that differ significantly from middle school. Understanding these expectations can help you prepare and adapt more effectively.

ACADEMIC EXPECTATIONS

Increased Workload: High school typically involves more homework, projects, and in-depth studies.

Higher Standards: The academic standards in high school are generally higher, with a greater emphasis on critical thinking and analysis.

Preparation for College or Career: High school is a key time for preparing for future educational or career goals. This includes considering college applications, standardized tests, and exploring potential career paths.

SOCIAL AND EXTRACURRICULAR EXPECTATIONS

Broader Social Dynamics: High school often brings a larger, more diverse student body. Navigating these new social waters can be both exciting and challenging.

Extracurricular Commitments: Participation in clubs, sports, and other activities is often more intense in high school and there are also more opportunities for leadership and specialization.

INDEPENDENCE AND RESPONSIBILITY

Self-Advocacy: High school students are expected to be more independent in managing their studies and seeking help when needed.

Time Management: Balancing academic, social, and personal responsibilities requires effective time management skills.

PERSONAL DEVELOPMENT

High school is a time for significant personal growth and self-discovery. Embrace this opportunity to learn more about who you are and what you want to achieve.

Understanding these expectations can help ease the transition to high school so you can approach this new chapter with confidence and enthusiasm.

REAL STORIES: PREPARING FOR THE NEXT BIG STEP

Let's explore stories of students preparing for high school in this section. These narratives illustrate how planning and seeking guidance can make the transition smoother.

STORY 1: SEEKING FAMILIAR FACES

After a few weeks of being in 9th grade, Fardowza started visiting her junior high assistant principal, regularly. She at first used the pretext of coming for candy, but soon confessed that things were different in high school and that she missed junior high. Though the assistant principal always welcomed her and the others who started coming (with a pass), he reminded them that their feelings of staying connected to the familiar was normal and that he'd always be there for them, but encouraged them to embrace the wonderful new things available in high school.

STORY 2: SETTING SMART GOALS

Mohammed had only recently arrived in the US from India, and though he spent the last semester in middle school, he was still nervous about going to high school. Seeking advice from his counselor, they worked together to help him establish some SMART goals. For starters, he was going to spend some time over the summer reading at least 5 books, exercising 3-5 times a week, keeping a daily journal, and listening to TED Talks about mastering your emotions.

STORY 3: FAMILIARIZING WITH THE SCHOOL ENVIRONMENT

Tatum wanted to become familiar with high school before the year started. He knew that there were a number of activities happening over the summer that could be easy excuses to show up and just hang out, maybe get to know a few people. He called the school and found out when football practices were and just started showing up. He would sit by the fence with his bike for a few practices reading the student handbook, but gradually he began moving closer, saying "hi" to the players. At times he would wander into the building and would start talking to anyone he saw until he felt quite comfortable going into 9th grade.

These short stories highlight that preparing for high school involves planning, setting goals, and familiarizing yourself with the new environment. Embracing the change with a proactive approach can lead to a successful transition.

ACTIVITIES AND REFLECTIONS

ACTIVITY 1: HIGH SCHOOL GOAL-SETTING

Create a list of goals you want to achieve in high school. Consider academic, extracurricular, and personal development goals.

ACADEMIC

-
-
-
-
-

EXTRACURRICULAR

-
-
-
-

PERSONAL DEVELOPMENT

-
-
-
-
-

REFLECTION 1: MIDDLE SCHOOL LESSONS

Reflect on the most valuable lessons you learned in middle school.

How can these lessons apply to your high school experience?

_____

_____

_____

_____

_____

_____

_____

_____

_____

_____

_____

_____

_____

_____

ACTIVITY 2: HIGH SCHOOL EXPECTATIONS BRAINSTORM

Brainstorm a list of your expectations for high school, both academically and socially. Compare this list with information from teachers, older students, or school resources to align your expectations with reality.

REFLECTION 2: PERSONAL GROWTH AREAS

Identify areas where you want to grow personally during high school. How will you work toward these areas of growth?

_____

_____

_____

_____

_____

_____

_____

_____

_____

_____

_____

_____

_____

_____

_____

_____

DOODLE CANVAS: LET YOUR PEN ROAM FREE!

Explore. Experiment. Express.

The focus of this guide is you! You can draw, write, paste your favorite stickers, or record special moments in this space. Make it reflect your individuality!

RESOURCE LIST

- **High School Transition Tips (Website):** Offers practical advice for transitioning to high school (www. transitioningtohighschool.org).
- **College Board:** Provides resources for college preparation, including information on AP courses and SATs (www. collegeboard.org).
- **TeenLife:** Lists extracurricular opportunities and summer programs for high school students (www.teenlife.com).
- **Mindset Works:** Has resources for developing a growth mindset, which is essential for adapting to new challenges (www.mindsetworks.com).

These resources offer guidance and support as you prepare for and transition into high school and can help you navigate this exciting new phase with confidence.

Chapter 10

Introduction to Staying Connected

- Overview of the importance of having a support network in middle school and beyond
- Emphasizing the value of connections for emotional and academic support

Utilizing Resources Within the School

- Identifying and making the most of available school resources, such as counselors, teachers, and clubs
- Tips on how to actively seek and use these resources for support and growth

Maintaining Connections with Mentors and Friends

- Strategies for keeping in touch with mentors and friends, especially after transitioning to high school or during other changes
- The role of these relationships in providing guidance and support

The Power of Networking

- Understanding networking and its importance
- Building and nurturing a network of supportive peers and adults

Real Stories: Starting Fresh

- Anonymized stories from students about adapting to new surroundings

Activities and Reflections

- Interactive exercises and journaling prompts focused on building and maintaining connections

Personalization Space and Resource Directory

- Space for students to note their experiences and strategies in building a support network
- A list of resources providing additional information on networking and building connections

CHAPTER TEN

STAYING CONNECTED

Even at your age, making strong and lasting connections with peers and adults in middle and high school can be beneficial. This chapter focuses on one of the most crucial aspects of your middle school journey and beyond: building and maintaining a strong support network.

Having a support network means more than just having friends. It includes mentors, teachers, family members, and anyone who provides guidance, encouragement, and assistance. These connections can be a source of advice and emotional support, and can even open doors to new opportunities.

In this chapter, we'll explore how to identify and connect with individuals who can be part of your support network. We'll discuss the importance of these relationships and how they can help you navigate challenges and contribute to your growth and success.

We'll also look at how to utilize the resources available within your school, learn how to maintain connections with mentors and friends, and the importance of networking. Building a strong support network is about creating a community that supports and uplifts you and that helps you thrive in middle school and beyond.

Let's dive into the ways you can stay connected and build a network that will accompany you through your educational journey and into the future.

UTILIZING RESOURCES WITHIN THE SCHOOL

Making the most of the resources available within your middle school or nearby high school is a key aspect of building a strong support network. Schools offer a variety of resources that can help you academically, socially, and emotionally.

Pro tip: Talking to family members or trusted adults about your goals can be quite meaningful, at this time.

ACADEMIC RESOURCES

Teachers: They are not just educators but also mentors who can provide academic guidance and support.

Tutoring Labs: Many schools offer tutoring services for students who need extra help.

Libraries: A great resource for research, studying, and finding books that interest you.

SOCIAL AND EMOTIONAL SUPPORT

School Counselors: They can offer advice on everything from academic pressure to personal issues.

Clubs and Groups: Joining clubs can connect you with peers who share your interests and provide a sense of belonging.

CAREER AND COLLEGE PLANNING

Guidance Offices: These can provide resources for exploring future careers and college options.

High School Counselors: They offer guidance on college applications, scholarships, and planning for post-high school education.

HOW TO ACCESS THESE RESOURCES

Don't hesitate to ask for help or information. Teachers and staff are there to support you.

Stay informed about the resources your school offers as they can change or expand over time.

Utilizing these school resources can enhance your educational experience, provide necessary support, and help build a foundation for your future goals.

MAINTAINING CONNECTIONS WITH MENTORS AND FRIENDS

Maintaining connections with mentors and friends, especially after transitioning to new environments like high school, is vital for ongoing support and guidance.

KEEPING IN TOUCH WITH MENTORS

Regular check-ins: Schedule periodic meetings or send updates to keep your mentors informed about your progress.

Seek advice: Don't hesitate to reach out for guidance on academic, social, or personal challenges.

STAYING CONNECTED WITH FRIENDS

Use technology: Social media, texting, and video calls can keep you connected even when physically apart.

Plan meet-ups: Regular get-togethers help maintain strong bonds.

THE ROLE OF THESE RELATIONSHIPS

Mentors can provide valuable advice and help open doors to new opportunities. Friends offer emotional support, understanding, and a sense of belonging.

These relationships form a crucial part of your support network and can offer different perspectives and support as you navigate various stages of your life.

> Pro tip: Don't get discouraged if a teacher, counselor, mentor, or friend doesn't respond the way you want them to right away. People are often in different places, so be patient and keep trying. Don't be bothersome, but check in from time to time.

THE POWER OF NETWORKING

Networking is more than just a business term; it's about building a web of relationships that can support and enrich your life, especially as you move through middle school and beyond.

UNDERSTANDING NETWORKING

Networking involves creating and maintaining connections with people who can offer advice, support, and opportunities.

It's about reciprocal relationships, where you also offer support and help to others in your network.

BUILDING YOUR NETWORK

Start with people you already know, like teachers, family, friends, and community members.

Attend school events, join clubs, go to youth groups, and participate in community activities to meet new people.

NURTURING YOUR NETWORK

Keep in touch with your connections through social media, emails, or occasional meet-ups.

Be genuine in your interactions and show interest in others' lives and experiences.

NETWORKING FOR FUTURE OPPORTUNITIES

Your network can provide valuable information about careers, colleges, internships, and other opportunities.

Remember, networking is a long-term investment. The connections you make now can benefit you in the future.

Networking helps in building a support system that can guide and assist you throughout your educational journey and into your career.

REAL STORIES: STARTING FRESH

In this final section, we look at stories of students adjusting to new environments. These narratives show the importance of seeking support and staying connected to old friends while embracing new opportunities.

STORY 1: REACHING OUT FOR SUPPORT

Mary graduated from 8th grade but transferred to another school for her freshman year. Naturally the adjustment was hard and at times she felt alone and scared. She decided to reach out to her friends from her old school and even emailed some of her old teachers. Her teachers and friends formed a bit of a support network for Mary by helping her to maintain old friendships and by advising her on how to adjust to the new school.

STORY 2: TURNING THINGS AROUND

Micah had a number of behavior infractions in middle school but wanted to turn things around in high school so that he could play basketball. He knew that it would be tough in this unfamiliar environment and very easy to fall back into his old ways. When he met with his counselor at freshman orientation, they discussed his concerns, and before he left for the night, the counselor had signed him up with an 11th grade mentor, and emailed the basketball coach to connect with him ASAP. Micah felt relieved and confident that things would be okay.

STORY 3: FINDING A NETWORK OF SUPPORT

Kaydence was a bit of an introvert in middle school and had a very small group of friends. She kept busy volunteering to help with the play, was part of the chess club, and the Battle of the Books club. She was quite anxious about going to high school because she didn't know what to expect and if she'd have the same opportunities as she did in middle school. To her great surprise, word had spread to the high school about her skill at playing chess, and volunteerism. She was immediately invited to an interest meeting for the chess club, and was given a warm welcome by the theater director to their first production. She soon realized she benefited from a network of support that had long been in place for students coming from middle school.

These narratives demonstrate that adjusting to new environments can be challenging, but with the right support and a proactive attitude, you can find your footing and thrive. Reaching out for help and staying connected to familiar faces can make the transition smoother and more enjoyable.

ACTIVITY 1: NETWORKING MAP

Create a map of your current network, including family, friends, teachers, and any other connections. Identify areas where you might want to expand your network.

REFLECTION 1: MENTOR IMPACT

Reflect on a mentor who has made a difference in your life. What have you learned from them? How can you apply these lessons going forward?

_____

_____

_____

_____

_____

_____

_____

_____

_____

_____

_____

_____

_____

_____

_____

_____

ACTIVITY 2: GOAL-ORIENTED NETWORKING

Think about your future goals and identify people in your network who could provide guidance or support in achieving these goals.

REFLECTION 2: RECIPROCITY IN RELATIONSHIPS

Consider how you can contribute to your relationships, not just what you can gain from them. How can you support your friends, mentors, or network connections?

_____

_____

_____

_____

_____

_____

_____

_____

_____

_____

_____

_____

_____

_____

_____

DOODLE CANVAS: LET YOUR PEN ROAM FREE!

Explore. Experiment. Express.

The focus of this guide is you! You can draw, write, paste your favorite stickers, or record special moments in this space. Make it reflect your individuality!

RESOURCE LIST

- **LinkedIn for Students:** A platform to connect with professionals and explore career opportunities (www.linkedin.com).

- **Toastmasters International:** A nonprofit educational organization that teaches public speaking and leadership skills through a worldwide network of clubs (www.toastmasters.org).

- **Future Business Leaders of America (FBLA):** Provides opportunities for high school students to develop business-related career competencies (www.fbla-pbl.org).

These resources can help you develop networking skills and provide platforms for building your support network, which is essential for your growth and success in middle school and beyond.

CONCLUSION

EMBRACING YOUR MIDDLE SCHOOL JOURNEY

As we close this guide, *Navigating Middle School: A Guide to Friendship, Growth, and Self-Discovery*, let's take a moment to reflect on the incredible journey you're on. Middle school is a unique adventure that is filled with new experiences, challenges, and growth opportunities.

Remember, middle school is your time to shine in your unique way. It's a time to explore who you are and who you want to be. You'll make new friends, learn new things, and face challenges that will make you stronger and wiser. Embrace every moment—the good, the not-so-good, and everything in between.

Amid this adventure, remember to find joy in the little things. A smile, a shared joke, a moment of wonder—these small joys can light up your days. Be kind and compassionate, not only to others but also to yourself. And amidst the hustle and bustle, hold onto the wisdom of your family, teachers, spiritual leader, and friends to remind you of the strength and courage within you, even on the toughest days.

Mistakes and challenges are part of every great story, and yours is no exception. They are not setbacks but setups for greater achievements and deeper understanding. Your middle school years are a canvas, and you hold the brush. Paint your story with bold strokes of perseverance, faith, and optimism.

As you turn each page of your middle school story, remember that you are never alone. You have a community of support around you and a faith that can move mountains. Carry the lessons from this guide in your heart and step forward with confidence and positivity.

Here's to your middle school journey—a journey of growth, joy, and self-discovery. May it be a beautiful testament to your strength, character, and faith.

Remember, the path may not always be clear or smooth, but each step brings new wisdom and strength.

Keep walking, keep learning!

www.ingramcontent.com/pod-product-compliance
Lightning Source LLC
Chambersburg PA
CBHW051309120626
46547CB00015B/2158